Purpose for Existence

Building a Sustainable Commitment to Excellence in Life

PURPOSE FOR EXISTENCE

By

ONIKOYI OLUSEGUN SAMUEL

CONTACT:

TEL: +2347030881810

FACEBOOK: OLUSEGUN ONIKOYI

EMAIL: SAMUELONIKOYI@HOTMAIL.COM

TABLE OF CONTENTS

INTRODUCTION

CHAPTER ONE

WHY AM I HERE ON EARTH

CHAPTER TWO

DISCOVERING YOUR PURPOSE FOR EXISTENCE

CHAPTER THREE

LACK OF PURPOSE FOR EXISTENCE (CHALLENGES FACED)

CHAPTER FOUR

SOLUTIONS TO OBSTACLES TO DISCOVERING PURPOSE FOR EXISTENCE

CHAPTER FIVE

QUOTES FOR PURPOSELESS LIFE

INTRODUCTION

Some people feel reluctant about pursuing the purpose for their existence because they worry that it sounds like selfish quest.However, true purpose is about recognizing your own gifts and using them to contribute to the world, whether those gifts are playing beautiful music for others to enjoy, helping friends and families solve problems, or simply bringing more joy into the lives of those around you. Your purpose consists of the central motivating aims. The reasons why you live.Purpose can guide life decisions, influence behavior, shape goals, offer a sense of direction, and create meaning. For some people, purpose is connected to vocation, meaningful, satisfying work. For others, theirs may lies in their responsibilities to their family or friends.Some people may find their purpose clearly expressed in all these aspects of life.

Purpose will be unique for everyone; what you identify as your path may be different from others. The reason for which something or someone exists. A lot of people in today's world are moving around without direction. If you do not seek to find, know and to understand the purpose of your life and the reason of your existence, you will continue to live by default, betraying yourself and thinking that it is okay to walk on a path that is not yours. A lot of times we develop this false belief that life is complicated and that the purpose of our lives is something very complex and hard to find, but that is not true. “What is my purpose in life? What is the reason of my existence?” it's something every human being should have clarity about.

Pursuing your purpose can sound quite scary, as it often involves taking risks and embracing a lot of new experiences. However, where you might normally be anxious or even afraid, you are more likely to feel calm or even blissful because you know that you are fulfilling your greatest potential, and have faith that you will succeed.

CHAPTER ONE

WHY AM I HERE ON EARTH

"WHY AM I HERE ON EARTH?" everyone has asked this question and I believe we would have gotten a lot of answer towards that.

It's a thing of consideration and we must take time to consider what our purpose is for being here on earth. Let me share with you somethings that helped me get meaning out of life.

When I was a child, I noticed I love teaching but not focusing on it. Before I graduated from secondary school, I had in mind to become a Military Officer. After I graduated from secondary school, for 3 years, I tried gaining admission into Nigeria Defense Academy, which didn't work out. The last exam I wrote in the year 2010, then, I met with a Naval Officer, he advised me that I should go to the school to study a course, when am through, I should put in for short service in the Military.

Then, I found myself in a cross road of making a life choice, a choice of destiny.I never had interest in a Civilian Institution, but I had no choice. After a long thought, I decided to study Computer Science in School, a part time course so as to get a job to assist myself in school.While studying, I tried my possible best in getting a good job, but all I got was a teaching job with low pay, but I decided to go for it because that was the only available job for me that moment. While teaching, I kept on looking for a better job which I didn't see. It was at this point in time I had the message of “DISCOVERING YOUR PURPOSE”.

I keyed to it, I stated praying, asking God for my purpose on earth. I saw so many revelations, that's when I knew I was a born teacher (my purpose). I discovered, there is a simple answer for the frequently asked question, "Why am I here on Earth?" There is a very simple answer, but it is understood only after we discover our purpose for existence.

If we can find the best possible answer to this question "Why am I here on Earth?", then we can live the best possible life. Everything around us has a purpose. Most of us can quickly tell what the purpose is for everything which we come in contact with. But when it comes to explaining our own purpose for existence, it is difficult, if not an impossible task.

Atheistic humanism claims that everything about us exists merely because of countless accidental evolutionary changes. If everything merely exists because of purposeless evolution, then the final product can have no meaningful purpose. If I am a product of an accident or series of accidents, then there would be no purpose except what I could make of my own life by my own power.

We live in a world that has been greatly influenced by the consequences of evolutionary thought. Evolution denies a purpose greater than self. Where there is no purpose greater than self, we are forced to live only for ourselves.

There are many people in this world who have been tricked into believing their purpose in life is to be "successful." Money is their goal. Accumulating the most things are important." For some "their goal is becoming the highest achiever". Becoming the most intelligent.Becoming the most beautiful. Finding the greatest pleasure.None of these goals will provide an adequate answer to the question, "Why am I here on Earth?" We know people who make things like success, beauty, money, or pleasure their primary motivating forces in life. If these worldly ambitions were desirable as primary goals, then, those people who make them their purpose for existence would be the happiest people in the world.

Those who have not discovered the purpose for existence, are the world's most miserable people, because they have no direction. Failure to discover the intended purpose for existence will cause them to suffer from the destructive consequences brought on by self-centeredness.Our schools fail to teach us a legitimate purpose for our existence. If we do not discover what our purpose for existence is, we will not be able to fulfill the purpose for which God intended when He created us. Those who are Christians are quick to reason that we exist for a purpose greater than self. Yet, can our acquaintances see that we live as if something besides ourselves is of the greatest importance to us? Do we appear to live by the world's standards? Have you chosen a purpose that is worthy of your best efforts? Have you chosen a purpose that will bring you the greatest happiness?

Let's examine few ideas from the Bible that will help us discover our PURPOSE FOR COMING INTO THIS WORLD.

- Romans 8:28 tells us that God knows what our purpose is. "And we know that all things work together for good to those who love God, to those who are the called according to His purpose." I believe that He has made our purpose clear in the Bible. He has revealed to us the answer to the question, "Why am I here on Earth?"

- In Isaiah 43:7, we can learn that God created us for His glory. We learn in John, chapter 17, that Jesus lived to glorify God. We want to be like Jesus Christ, we also should live such that our lives glorify God. We can correctly conclude that the purpose for our existence is to GLORIFY GOD WITH WHAT HAD BEEN ENDOWERED IN US.

But this is not the simple answer, I said we can discover for the question "Why am I here on Earth?" For one might now ask, "How do I know what I have been endowered with?"Jesus makes it clear in John 4:34 that His purpose for being on the earth was to do the will of God. If we want to find the happiness that Jesus our Savior had, then we, too, must be committed to doing the will of God. When we do His will, God is glorified. So, "How do we glorify God?" By doing His will.Irrespective of who you are, even if you are trying your best, it can be predicted that there will be times when you will fail to do God's will. Nevertheless, God is glorified when we keep trying to do His will even after our failures.

Consider the parable of the talents in Matthew

25:14-30: "For the kingdom of heaven is like a man traveling to a far country, who called his own servants and delivered his goods to them. And to one he gave five talents, to another two, and to another one, to each according to his own ability; and immediately he went on a journey. Then he who had received the five talents went and traded with them, and made another five talents. And likewise, he who had received two gained two more also. But he who had received one went and dug in the ground, and hid his lord's money. After a long time, the lord of those servants came and settled accounts with them. So, he who had received five talents came and brought five other talents, saying, `Lord, you delivered to me five talents; look, I have gained five more talents besides them.' His lord said to him, `Well done, good and faithful servant; you were faithful over a few things, I will make you ruler over many things. Enter into the joy of your lord.' He also who had received two talents came and said, `Lord, you delivered to me two talents; look, I have gained two more talents besides them.' His lord said to him, `Well done, good and faithful servant; you have been faithful over a few things, I will make you ruler over many things. Enter into the joy of your lord.' Then he who had received the one talent came and said, `Lord, I knew you to be a hard man, reaping where you have not sown, and gathering where you have not scattered seed. And I was afraid, and went and hid your talent in the ground. Look, there you have what is yours.' But his lord answered and said to him, `You wicked and lazy servant, you knew that I reap where I have not sown, and gather where I have not scattered seed. Therefore, you ought to have deposited my money with the bankers, and at my coming I would have received back my own with interest. Therefore, take the talent from him, and give it to him who has ten talents. For to everyone who has, more will be given, and he will have abundance; but from him who does not have, even what he has will be taken away. And cast the unprofitable servant into the outer darkness. There will be weeping and gnashing of teeth.'

This story is about 3 servants. Two of them had discovered how to please their master through their gift to him. One was unprofitable, not having learned how to serve or how to submit to the will of the master. Most of the problem seems to be related to the unprofitable servant's failure to know his master, as shown in verses 24 & 25. We can acceptably serve God only by getting to know Him. We can please God only by discovering through His Word what he had endowed into us, what He wants us to do and what He wants us to be.

So, we can conclude that to please God and have a meaningful and happy life, we must live to serve God through is word and doing His will to fulfill the purpose for our existence.

Many honest people would now ask, "Why should I be interested in glorifying, pleasing, or serving God?" As we mature as Christians, we find the answer to the question, "What's in it for me?", to be of little importance. But God surely provides a simple answer to explain to the Christian and non-Christian alike why we would even consider serving Him. When many of us became Christians, we were acting out of fear. Frankly, we were afraid of going to Hell. This is not bad that our initial motivation was fear. People can be shaped by force through fear. Fear is probably necessary for the beginning of wisdom. But, fear of the wrath of God is not an adequate motivating force that can be sustained throughout a lifetime. Fear of failure will not properly motivate us to strive for Heaven. Eventually fear produces rebellion and alienation and frustration. Human nature resists and resents fear and force. People do not have to be controlled by fear and force. Christians, who are not mature beyond the stage of serving God out of fear, will not find the happiness which God has promised to those who serve Him whole heartedly.

The force which moves us away from fear and also provides us with a satisfactory answer to the question "why serve God?" is LOVE. Love is the only alternative to fear and force.

- I John 4:18 says, "Love casts out fear." Love doesn't come naturally. We must learn how to love. After we learn how to love, then we will

want to do what we ought to do in spite of our failures.

WHAT IS LOVE?

Jesus answered this question beautifully in the parable of the Good Samaritan. (Luke 10:25.) “And behold, a certain lawyer stood up and tested Jesus, saying, "Teacher, what shall I do to inherit eternal life?" “Jesus said to him, `What is written in the law? What is your reading of it?"“So, the lawyer answered and said, `You shall love the Lord your God with all your heart, with all your soul, with all your strength, and with your entire mind,' and `your neighbor as yourself.'" “And Jesus said to him, `You have answered rightly; do this and you will live.” Many people, like this lawyer, have chosen to try to love God without getting involved with anyone else.Luke

10:29, “But the lawyer, wanting to justify himself, said to Jesus, `and who is my neighbor?” People were always trying to get our Savior distracted from teaching about the two main themes of each of His lessons: Love God and love others, which Jesus called the greatest and second greatest commandments in Matt. 22:37-40.)

Luke 10:30-37: Then Jesus answered and said: “A certain man went down from Jerusalem to Jericho, and fell among thieves, who stripped him of his clothing, wounded him, and departed, leaving him half dead. Now by chance a certain priest came down that road. And when he saw him, he passed by on the other side. Likewise, a Levite, when he arrived at the place, came and looked, and passed by on the other side. But a certain Samaritan, as he journeyed, came where he was. And when he saw him, he had compassion on him, and went to him and bandaged his wounds, pouring on oil and wine; and he set him on his own animal, brought him to an inn, and took care of him. On the next day, when he departed, he took out two denarii, gave them to the innkeeper, and said to him, `Take care of him; and whatever more you spend, when I come again, I will repay you.' So, which of these three do you think was neighbour to him who fell among the thieves?" And the lawyer said, "He who showed mercy on *him." Then Jesus said to him, "Go and do likewise."*

Note in verse 37 that the Samaritan fulfilled the command of "Love thy neighbour as thyself" when he "showed mercy." He demonstrated his love. Which do you think God considers more important: what we think and say or what we do? We can prove our love only by our actions.Would my wife be pleased when I said, "I love you," but every day I also hit her? Our actions show whether we really love someone or not. Attending every worship service is important, but your presence here does not prove to me or to God or to anyone else that you love God, though we sometimes try to fool ourselves into thinking so.

God cannot be pleased by formal worship alone. He said, "I have had enough of your worship," in Isaiah 1:11. It is all meaningless unless we love God enough to serve Him.

In Matthew 21:28-30, Jesus said, A man had two sons, and he came to the first and said, `Son, go, work today in my vineyard.' He answered and said, `I will not,' but afterward he regretted it and went. Then the father came to the second and said likewise. And the son answered and said, `I go, sir,' but he did not go."

The first son demonstrated his love by his actions.

The second son gave lip service without doing anything to please his father. We must be careful, else, we will think that through our worship services we are serving God, when it may be nothing but lip service from God's point of view.

We must learn to serve God because of our love for Him. Now, a question that deserves an answer is, "Why love God?" Why do you love God? Why should others love God? Here is the answer I can think of. "For God so loved you that He gave His only begotten Son, that if you believe in Him, you should not perish but have everlasting life." In Romans 5:8 we read, "But God demonstrates His own love toward us, in that while we were still sinners, Christ died for us."I love God because He first loved me. He has not merely claimed to love us, but He has proved His love for us. When I recognize the love God has for me, I cannot but respond with love in return.The most remarkable thing about God's love is that it is totally unconditional. The Bible teaches me that no matter what I am or what I do in this life, I know that God will love me. I cannot help but respond to this. This sort of love makes me want to serve God. It makes me want to please God. It makes me want to glorify God. I don't have to be forced to do the things that I should.

The simplest answer to the question I asked at the beginning of the lesson, “Why am I here on Earth?" is that “I WAS CREATED TO LOVE GOD AND TO DO HIS WILL”. I can find no simpler answer to the search for my purpose for existence. Without love, "I am nothing," Paul wrote in I Corinthians 13:2.Now that we have established that LOVE AND WILL is our purpose for existence, we must learn to love the way we should and make His will our goal. I Corinthians 14:1 says, “Make love your aim." We must make all other goals of lesser significance in our lives.

“If you love me, keep my commandments,” Jesus tells us in John 14:15. We have likely all been guilty at some point in our lives of trying to keep the commandments as if they were the principal concept in this verse. Jesus is telling us that obedience will be the result of our love. Love will not be the result of our obedience. We prove our love by our actions. But we cannot offer our actions as proof of our love.When we get the order of things reversed in John 14:15, we get our goals and our rewards confused. If love is our primary goal, then we can't make going to Heaven our purpose. We must get our perspective straight; Heaven is our reward. Learn to serve God because you love God, and because He loves you.In Colossians 3:23 & 24 we read, “And whatever you do, do it heartedly, as to the Lord and not to men, knowing that from the Lord you will receive the reward of the inheritance; for you serve the Lord.”

Let us mature beyond the idea that we are serving God so that we can go to Heaven. Understand that your goal is different from your reward. Out of love, we learn to serve God even as if it doesn't matter whether Heaven exists or not.

To help you understand this better, whenever I had opportunity to speak to people, I always tell of a scenario of a child that is been sent to the market by the parent. Every parent will always give a list of what is expected of their child to do in the market. But, when we were all sent into this world, we were not given a list of what to do from heaven, but we had a blue print of our life designed by God, which is expected of us to accomplish on earth.

Systematically, when we got to this world, we all forget that, we had a master plan of what we are here to do on earth and the only way to know this,is asking from our creator (God) the content in our life manual.Living outside the will of God, working outside God's plan for our life, is totally a failure to our existence, because, everything we are going to become, our success in life; had been written down in our life manual.

The solution to our life hustling and struggling, is finding out from God what had been written about us.If we focus on the purpose for our existence, we will understand that our goal in life must be to love God and to do His will. The Bible makes it very clear that we demonstrate our love for God when we do His will.

Men and women, who pursue happiness, without discovering they exist for a purpose, find nothing but emptiness. If you have been seeking the wrong goals, now is time to change. Though change can be painful at first, when we seek to glorify, serve, please, and love God, He will provide a peace that surpasses all understanding. Let God fill the void that is in your life. If you have never surrendered to God's will, He requires that after you believe that Jesus is who He said He is, you must turn from your sinful ways that lead to destruction. Then you must be buried in water as Jesus was buried in the grave. Then as Christ was raised up without the sin for which He died, so, too, will you become a new creature having God's forgiveness.If you have obeyed the Gospel, but now find yourself back in the realm of the lost, remember that God loves you no matter what your sin. He will forgive you if you repent and ask for His forgiveness and never go back to sin anymore. He promised we can have an abundant life even before we get to Heaven. The rewards start now.

Don't let another day go by without pleasing your Creator (God).

CHAPTER TWO

DISCOVERING YOUR PURPOSE FOR EXISTENCE

Every human being was created for a purpose. The purpose of existence is the ultimate goal of one's being. It can also be defined as one's calling or vocation.

The purpose of one's existence is what defines the person. It's in fact, the essence of one's existence. Life without a purpose is a life without direction.The happiest and the most fulfilled ones on earth are those who discovered their purpose for existence and were able to actualize their mission here on earth. Before the end of this reflection, you must discover the purpose for your existence and allow God to give you the grace to actualize it.God did not create man by chance. Man was not a product of accident. Before creating man, God had a plan and a purpose for him. In the book of

Genesis 1:26 the Lord God said, "Let us make man in our image, according to our likeness; and let them have dominion over the fish of the sea, and over the birds of the air, and over the cattle, and over all the wild animals of the earth, and over every creeping thing that creeps upon the earth."

Man was the only animal that was created in God's image and likeness. Although he was the last and the most vulnerable animal in the order of creation, yet, out of love God placed him over and above every other thing He created. Man was given the authority to govern the entire creation. The psalmist was amazed at the enviable position where God placed man. Reflecting on the glorious position of man in the order of creation,

Psalm 8 declares, "What are human beings that you are mindful of them, mortals that you care for them? Yet you have made them a little lower than God, and crowned them with glory and honour. You have given them dominion over the works of your hands; you have put all things under their feet, all sheep and oxen, and also the beasts of the field, the birds of the air, and the fish of the sea, whatever passes along the paths of the seas."

Unfortunately, man did not even know that he is a being with a difference. Some men have even reduced themselves lower than inanimate things by worshipping idols, the work of human hands. Our Lord Jesus Christ was the first man that discovered the purpose for his existence. He knew clearly why he came into the world (Luke 4:18). "The Spirit of the Lord is upon me, because he hath anointed me to preach the gospel to the poor; He hath sent me to heal the brokenhearted, to preach deliverance to the captives and recovering of sight to the blind to set at liberty them that are bruised" And within a short period of his life, he was able to actualize the purpose for his existence. Most of the great prophets in the bible did not know the purpose for their existence.

As God tries to reveal the purpose for their existence, they were surprise.Some of them even doubted the purpose for their existence. For instance, when God told Moses that he was destined to liberate the Israelites from bondage, he asked, "Who am I that I should go to Pharaoh, and bring the Israelites out of Egypt?"

(Exodus 3:11). "And Moses said unto God, who am I, that I should go unto Pharaoh, and that I should bring forth the children of Israel out of Egypt? ... 14. And God said unto Moses, I Am That I Am: and he said, thus shalt thou say unto the children of Israel, I Am hath sent me unto you".

Moses saw himself as nobody but in the sight of God, he was a great liberator. God used a lot of signs and wonders to prove to Moses that he was not just an ordinary human being. He was a destined child.The moment Moses discovered the purpose for his life, he lived a fulfilled life. At a stage, he was even the one encouraging his fellow Israelites. When the Egyptians were matching forward to attack them, he told his people, "Do not be afraid, stand firm, and see the deliverance that the LORD will accomplish for you today; for the Egyptians whom you see today you shall never see again. The LORD will fight for you, and you have only to keep still." Imagine, this is the same Moses that thought he was nobody! When he finally discovered the purpose for his existence he was now speaking like a warrior. Child of God, from today God will transform your life from nobody to somebody. He will use you to deliver your people from bondage.

When God called the Prophet Jeremiah, he revealed to him the purpose for his existence. He said, "Before I formed you in the womb, I knew you, and before you were born, I consecrated you; I appointed you a prophet to the nations." Jeremiah was surprise and even afraid. He exclaimed: "Ah, Lord GOD! Truly I do not know how to speak, for I am only a boy." But the LORD said to me, "Do not say, 'I am only a boy'; for you shall go to all to whom I send you, and you shall speak whatever I command you.Do not be afraid of them, for I am with you to deliver you, says the LORD." Child of

God, I may not know your age. But even if you are as young a Jeremiah the Lord will use you to deliver your nation. As a child of God, you are not just ordinary, you are indeed a prophet to the nation!

When the Lord called Gideon, he said to him through an angel, "The LORD is with you, you are a mighty warrior." Gideon answered him, "But sir, if the LORD is with us, why then has all this happened to us? And where are all his wonderful deeds that our ancestors recounted to us, saying, 'Did not the LORD bring us up from Egypt?' But now the LORD has cast us off, and given us into the hand of the Midianites. "Then the LORD turned to him and said, "Go in this might of yours and deliver Israel from the hand of Midian; I hereby commission you."He responded, "But sir, how can I deliver Israel? My clan is the weakest in Manasseh, and I am the least in my family. "The LORD said to him, "But I will be with you, and you shall strike down the Midianites, every one of them."

Child of God, even if you are from the minority group or weakest clan as in the case of Gideon, God will still use you to deliver your people from bondage. When God is involved, your family background does not really matter. God will use you to humiliate the Midianites of your generation. He will use you to silence the fools.

The call of Peter was an interesting one. It has something to do with divine vocation and breakthrough. Before Peter finally discovered the purpose for his life, he spent most of his life as an ordinary fisherman. He was actually laboring in vain until the very day when he encountered Jesus Christ, the Destiny changer. Jesus said to him.

"Put out into the deep water and let down your nets for a catch." Simon answered, "Master, we have worked all night long but have caught nothing.Yet if you say so, I will let down the nets." When they had done this, they caught so many fish that their nets were beginning to break. So, they signaled their partners in the other boat to come and help them. And they came and filled both boats, so that they began to sink. But when Simon Peter saw it, he fell down at Jesus' knees, saying, "Go away from me, Lord, for I am a sinful man!"

Child of God, even if you are a sinner, like Peter, there is still hope for you! As Jesus is stepping into the boat of your life your destiny will change! Your business will flourish.You will start recording success in your academics and career.

<u>CHAPTER THREE</u>

LACK OF PURPOSE FOR EXISTENCE

(CHALLENGES FACED)

Having clear direction in life, helps you achieve and fulfill your purpose. Trials and challenges are bound to occur, but you don't give up during difficult situations, and when you perceive obstacles in life, it serves as an opportunity to grow and learn.Having a life purpose is really important for your wellness, achievements and growth in your existence. When someone is lacking this purpose, they often feel that their life lacks fulfillment and they might experience an existential crisis.

CHALLENGES FACED WITH LACK OF PURPOSE

- If you feel like your life has no meaning and direction, things like decision-making, future planning, maintaining or forming relationships and choosing a career can all become very difficult situations.
- Many times, lack of purpose can trigger depression, anxiety and fear, as your uncertainty and sense of feeling lost can be overwhelming.Here are some symptoms that you might experience if you lack purpose in life:

- Feeling of demotivated to try new things, and don't know what really matters to you.
- Feeling of things not working the way it should be.
- Anxiousness and anxiety of thinking about the future.
- Struggle to make clear decisions in life. Fear of the future.
- Wondering what life is bringing toward you.

OBSTACLES TO DISCOVERING PURPOSE FOR EXISTENCE

If discovering life purpose were easy, everyone would have already done it. It is important to be patient with the process and let it unfold. If you are struggling to clarify your life purpose, ask yourself if you are:

1. Overlooking the value of an interest, skill or passion, taking it for granted and assuming everyone has it. We often overlook things that we do on a day-to-day basis, or because it has been part of our role or duty within our family or work.
2. Insisting that everyone's life purpose is completely unique and profound. It is normal for many people to want the same things out of life.

A life purpose does not have to be world changing or profound but specific to you, however wide ranging.

3. Feeling the pressure. Everyone is so busy these days and the financial pressures in people's lives can be very real. Perhaps it is possible to find a transitional state, a role that will pay the bills but not take up 100% of time and energy. Most people will not be fulfilled and satisfied in their work until it becomes an expression of their life purpose.
4. Thinking that a life purpose is only for special people. Everyone has a purpose, not just artists, writers, musicians and religious leaders.

CHAPTER FOUR

SOLUTIONS TO OBSTACLES TO DISCOVERING PURPOSE FOR EXISTENCE

1. Take time and steps to change your life and become healthier and happier. If you are unsatisfied with an aspect of your live, that means you need to create change in your actions and doings.

2. Identify any negative thoughts that keep you stuck from moving forwards with your life. Often times we are our own meanest critic. Negative thoughts train our brains to see negative situations, rather than positive ones. A helpful step to changing this behavior is positive self-talk. Every time you have a negative thought about yourself, try to come up with two positive things in which you like about yourself or your life.

3. Explore what career path you are convinced or led about and would make you feel fulfilled. Career fulfillment can give you a greater sense of purpose in the world; therefore, it is important to make sure you love what you are doing! If you are unhappy with an aspect of your job, try to find a way to incorporate things that make you feel good about the work you are doing.

4. Learn how to make use of your skills and experiences. Each of us are unique and therefore holds unique abilities. If you are someone who enjoys public speaking, find a way to do more of it! Not everyone has the same skills as you, and it is important to remember you bring personalized experiences to the table that nobody else can offer!

5. Formulate a set of achievable goals and a plan of action. Having a list of goals is a good way to remind yourself that you are making progress. Large changes are more difficult to see as they take a long time to complete. So, breaking these changes into steps can make you feel more motivated, and successful. And it shall be well with you in Jesus mighty name, Amen!

CHAPTER FIVE

QUOTE FOR

PURPOSELESS LIFE

- Life without purpose, is time without meaning, effort without result.
- Activity without purpose is the drain of your life. The greatest tragedy in life is not death, but a life without a clear purpose.
- Without a purpose, life is motion without meaning, activity without direction, and events without reason.
- A life without a positive purpose, is an unnecessary gamble with no positive possibility.
- Life without a defined purpose is similar to a boat without a crew in the middle of the ocean.
- Without sense of purpose and clear direction of your life, you will only be building a fake brand of you.
- Without God, life has no purpose, and without purpose, life has no meaning. Without meaning, life has no significance or hope.

- The kind of death you should mourn over is the one that happen when you abort your potential prematurely! - Life without purpose is a tragedy!
- We need both to aspire and accomplish. Without a vision for your life, without a sense of purpose, you will begin to die a slow death.
- To have meaning, our lives require both passion and purpose. A life without passion is like a furnace without fuel, and without purpose, like a ship without a rudder.
- Efforts and courage are not enough without purpose and direction.
- When you walk in purpose, you collide with destiny.
- Discovering Purpose for Existence is what gives life a meaning.

The End.

www.ingramcontent.com/pod-product-compliance
Lightning Source LLC
LaVergne TN
LVHW020536160826
845677LV00015B/4083

* 9 7 9 8 8 4 7 1 1 0 5 9 4 *